MEET THE CHARACTERS

Dave Clark is a fun-loving kid with some extraordinary challenges. He had a disease called polio so he uses crutches and braces on his legs to help him walk. But can that stop Dave from being extraordinary?

Duke is Dave's goofy dog. He's a boxer mix and he's always up for joining in the fun.

Ernie Pound is a classmate of Dave's who's ready and willing to lend a hand.

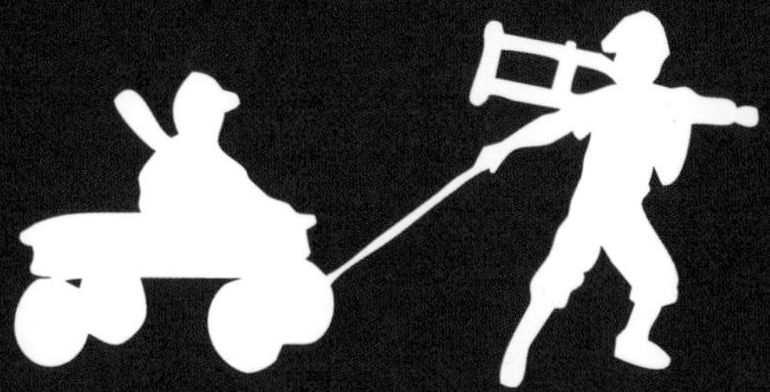

www.mascotbooks.com

A Pound of Kindness

For more information, please contact:
Mascot Books
620 Herndon Parkway #320
Herndon, VA 20170
info@mascotbooks.com

Library of Congress Control Number: 2018909840

CPSIA Code: PRT1218A
ISBN-13: 978-1-68401-769-0

Illustrations created in Adobe PhotoShop and Clip Studio Paint
Typeset in 16/22 Museo

Printed in the United States

A Pound of Kindness

BY DOUG CORNFIELD

ILLUSTRATED BY MARK BRAYER

DAVE CLARK WAS AN ACTIVE LITTLE KID.

He liked eating donuts. He liked playing with trains and his crazy dog, Duke. More than anything, he liked playing sports with his younger brothers and friends from the neighborhood.

But there was something different about Dave. He had braces on his legs and walked with crutches.

Dave grew up in the 1950s. During that time many people caught a serious disease called polio. When Dave was a baby, he got really sick with this disease. He spent days and nights away from his family in a hospital where he received special attention from doctors and nurses to help him recover.

As he got older, Dave realized his legs didn't work as well as other kids' legs. He couldn't jump as high or run as fast, but he tried his best not to let that hold him back. With the help of his braces and crutches, he could do a lot of things. He just did them a little differently.

Dave went to school like everyone else. He was in the first grade and he liked his teacher, Mrs. Lewis. He liked the crafts they did. He especially loved going outside to play at recess.

ONE DAY AT SCHOOL,

Mrs. Lewis made a big announcement — they were going on a field trip! Dave was so excited. What would they see? Would they go to a museum with cool dinosaurs? Would they go to the Baseball Hall of Fame?

"We'll be visiting the firefighters and fire trucks at the firehouse!" Mrs. Lewis announced. "It's right down the street, so we'll all walk there together. Won't that be fun?"

The kids couldn't wait.

"SHINY RED ENGINES!"
"BIG RED HATS!"
"TALL SLIDEY POLES!"

But Dave wasn't excited. The walk from the school to the firehouse was all he could think about. He had his own style of walking: throwing his feet out in front of him, then catching up to them with his crutches. It was hard work and it took a lot of energy. He had it down to a rhythm, but he still struggled to keep up with his classmates.

Dave was worried.

WHAT IF HE HAD TO TAKE A BREAK AND THE WHOLE CLASS HAD TO WAIT FOR HIM?

He couldn't imagine anything worse.

The next week, all Dave did was worry. When his classmates talked about the firehouse, he worried.

When Mrs. Lewis showed pictures of the firehouse, he worried.

When his parents talked about how nice the weather would be for a walk, Dave worried. His heart beat fast and his mouth felt dry. He didn't want to go to school anymore.

The night before the field trip, Dave told his parents he couldn't go to school the next day.

"Why not?" his mom asked.

"Because I don't like firehouses," Dave said.

"How do you know if you've never been to one?" his dad asked. "You'll enjoy it, Dave. Now eat your dinner, please."

After dinner, Dave went to his room to get ready for bed. He couldn't stop worrying about the next day.

"Dukey boy," he said to his dog, "why aren't you bigger? If you were bigger, I could ride you to the firehouse. We'd be the first ones to get there."

Duke nudged Dave's legs playfully. It gave Dave an idea!

"That's it, Duke!" said Dave, taking off his braces and waving them in Duke's face. "Chew on these! Then I won't be able to walk at all."

But all Duke did was roll over so Dave could pet his belly with the crutch.

Dave sighed. "If only my braces were covered in bacon..."

When Dave woke up the morning of the field trip, he tried to convince his mom that he couldn't go.

"I'M SICK," he said. "COUGH, COUGH."

"You're not," said his mom. "Out of bed, please."

Dave coughed again. "But Mom, I'll get all the other kids sick."

"You won't," said his mom. "Braces on, now! You are not going to be late."

When Dave got to school, everyone else was so excited. They rushed back and forth, looking for their friends to walk with. But Dave just stood off to the side, leaning on his crutches, dreading what was to come.

Everybody found their place in line. The class was ready to set off. Dave took a deep breath from his spot at the very end. Just as he was about to take his first step, he heard an unfamiliar sound. And then a voice.

RUMBLE, RUMBLE, RUMBLE.

"HOP IN, DAVE!
I'll pull you along!"

Dave couldn't believe it! His classmate Ernie Pound was pulling a bright red Radio Flyer wagon behind him!

Without a second thought, Dave hopped into the wagon, tucked in his crutches, and Ernie began pulling him along.

"LOOK!" John called. "There goes Dave and Ernie!"

"Wow!" cried Peggie. "I want to pull the wagon too!"

"Me too!" D.J. shouted. "Can we all pull Dave along?"

"That sounds like a great idea," said Mrs. Lewis.

Everyone took turns pulling Dave in Ernie's shiny red wagon. Dave knew why it was called a Radio Flyer because he felt like he was really flying!

They arrived at the firehouse, ready for their visit. Dave turned to Ernie and said, "Thanks, Ernie. I couldn't have done it without you."

Side by side, Dave and Ernie walked through the firehouse. They met the firefighters and saw the fire trucks.

They even got to ring the bell and watch the firefighters slide down the pole!

"I want to do that one day!" said Dave.

"Me too," said Ernie.

All too soon, it was time to leave the station. As the class filed out, Dave and Ernie looked for their shiny red wagon. The firefighters had parked it next to the shiny red fire trucks. It fit right in!

The fire chief held out his hand. "Put 'er there."

Dave shook it proudly.

"That's quite a handshake you have there, young man. Looks like Fire Chief Ernie's ready to pull you along! See you next time!"

Everyone took turns pulling Dave back to school. Some pulled him fast, some pulled him slow. No matter what, Dave still felt like he was flying.

"YOUNG DAVE CLARK NEVER FORGOT THE KINDNESS OF ERNIE POUND."

THE DAVE & ERNIE STORY

Dave Clark never forgot the kindness of Ernie Pound and thanked him from the bottom of his heart in his book, *Diamond in the Rough: The Dave Clark Story.* But Dave always wished he could thank Ernie in person for his selfless act of kindness. The only problem was the pair hadn't seen each other since elementary school!

Dave's friend Doug Cornfield was so touched by the story that he set off on a mission. After some research and digging, Doug found Ernie Pound, reached out, and asked him to come to one of Dave's book signings.

The day of the signing, Ernie waited in line to see Dave like everyone else. When Ernie made it to the front of the line and Dave asked who to sign the book to, Ernie just said, "Ernie Pound." The room instantly filled with emotion. With tears in his eyes, Dave shook Ernie's hand and then embraced him. Dave finally got to thank Ernie face to face.

There is more to the story! You see, Dave Clark is the only professional baseball player to pitch from crutches, and he soon learned that Ernie Pound had become an accomplished pitcher in his own right. Ernie is a professional horseshoe thrower who has placed second and fifth in world level competitions.

Today Dave Clark and Doug Cornfield recognize unsung heroes like Ernie with the "Pulling Each Other Along" award. The kindness Ernie showed Dave inspired this award and it has been given to many people throughout the years. Ernie is, of course, an esteemed "Pulling Each Other Along" award winner.

ABOUT DISABILITY, DREAM, AND DO

The Disability, Dream, and Do (D3Day) sports camps were created by Dave Clark and Doug Cornfield. Dave is the only pitcher in professional sports history to pitch on crutches, and Doug Cornfield is a former NCAA medal winning runner at the University of Georgia. Doug also has a child who was born with neither arm fully developed. The D3Day camps allow professional players to interact with children with special needs in various

drills and compete in sports with no limitations. In 2016, Dave Stevens, who was born without legs yet played college football and minor league baseball, came on board as the D3Day camps expanded to other cities in the US. Dave, Dave, and Doug now run camps all over the country and share their amazing stories as well as inspire others to look past a disability and turn it into an ability instead.

Learn more at d3day.com.

ABOUT THE AUTHOR

Doug J. Cornfield, Sr. is an author, speaker, and former college athlete. He is the director of the Disability, Dream, and Do (D3Day) sports camps, created with Dave Clark. In college he was a top contender in track and field, and a scholarship athlete at the University of Georgia. His professional experience includes time spent in both the family entertainment industry and as a senior financial advisor for Merrill Lynch. More recently, he partnered with Dave Clark to organize their company and run D3Day events, where the duo creates opportunities for children and young adults with special needs to interact with professional sports players and compete with no limitations. Doug is married to Jackie and their family includes seven children, one of whom was born with neither arm fully developed, and three grandchildren.

ABOUT THE ILLUSTRATOR

Mark Brayer has been working in the creative business for many years. Most of his professional work is made up of illustrating books for various publishers and authors. Other projects include creating illustrated characters for educational materials, websites, logos, t-shirts, and comic books. For the last five years, he has been creating original licensed posters for CBS Studios' Star Trek franchise, and a poster collection of NASA and space-themed art. He lives just south of Indianapolis, Indiana, with his wife Danni and his daughter Hayley.

ABOUT DAVE & DUKE

I have been traveling with Dave Clark for many years now. He tells me that I know his story better than he does. When I started thinking about writing *A Pound of Kindness*, I realized I didn't quite know everything so I began asking Dave more detailed questions about his youth. One of those questions was whether or not he had a dog growing up. Without hesitation, he said he had a dog whose name was Duke, a boxer mix of some sort. *Great!* I thought. *A dog is a perfect way to help convey the message of kindness in a children's book.*

Fast forward to when we finished the cover for this book, which of course features Duke. After the cover reveal, I received a text message from one of Dave's cousins, Vicki, who knew I was working on the story. Her message included a photo of Dave and Duke! Even more amazing was that Duke looked strikingly similar to the Duke drawn by Mark Brayer, the book's illustrator.

Naturally, I shared this photo with Dave who had absolutely no memory of it. He even thought I had edited a dog into an old photo of him to play a joke. But no, it's a real photo taken of Dave and the real Duke, presumably by Dave's parents long ago. It's almost as if they knew we were going to write a children's book about their incredible son and his faithful friend. And they were right.

-Doug Cornfield